Wisdom for Marriage

Boyd Bailey

Cover designed by truth in advertising
© Copyright 2014 Wisdom Hunters, LLC
Published by Wisdom Hunters, LLC
http://www.wisdomhunters.com
Book ISBN: 978-0615873824

INTRODUCTION

God is love. He is the love standard for serious followers of Jesus Christ. These 30 devotionals on love are designed to lead us into a deeper love relationship with our heavenly Father. It is Christ's greatest command, thus there is no greater goal for Christians than to be loved by God and to love God. His love is lovely and lingers long.

These writings are meant to move us from settling for a mediocre love that only loves expecting something in return—to an unselfish love that flows from being thoroughly loved by the Lord. His love loves in a radical way—way beyond the world's way. Do you invite Jesus to soothe your soul with the warm embrace of His eternal love? Does your love flow from His love? A daily love relationship with the Lord is wise.

"Let the morning bring me word of your unfailing love, for I have put my trust in you. Show me the way I should go, for to you I entrust my life" (Psalm 143:8).

Jesus knew an effective evangelism strategy for a lost world is the love we have for one another. "By this everyone will know that you are my disciples, if you love one another" (John 15:35). Can you imagine how many of the unloved lost would be saved if all believers loved well? The early church modeled enthusiastically God's eternal love.

"Every day they continued to meet together in the temple courts. They broke bread in their homes and ate together with glad and sincere hearts, praising God and enjoying the favor of all the people. And the Lord added to their number daily those who were being saved" (Acts 2:46-47).

I don't always love well. I don't feel like it, I'm mad, I'm worried or I question God. Notice the five personal pronouns in the last two sentences. It reminds me that when I am the focus, my love for God and people do not get the attention they deserve. When I struggle to love, I must first take a step back, die to my desires and submit to Christ.

It's in His loving arms that we are reminded of what authentic love feels like. Its depth is much deeper than the most loving relationship on earth. Its breadth of influence is wider that the most loving people group in the world. God's love never runs out, it only runs on robustly and freely. Nothing, nothing, nothing can separate us from God's love!

"Who shall separate us from the love of Christ? Shall trouble or hardship or persecution or famine or nakedness or danger or sword? As it is written: "For your sake we face death all day long; we are considered as sheep to be slaughtered." No, in all these things we are more than conquerors through him who loved us. For I am convinced that neither death nor life, neither angels nor demons, neither the present nor the future, nor any powers, neither height nor depth, nor anything else in all creation, will be able to separate us from the love of God that is in Christ Jesus our Lord" (Romans 8:35-39).

As my loving Grandmother told me right after I became a Christian, "Boyd talk much about the love of God, because love never fails!"

OTHER BOOKS BY BOYD BAILEY

Seeking Daily the Heart of God, Volume I – a 365-day Devotional
Seeking Daily the Heart of God, Volume II – a 365-day Devotional
Infusion – a 90-day Devotional
Seeking God in the Psalms – a 90-day Devotional
Seeking God in the Proverbs – a 90-day Devotional
Wisdom for Graduates – a 30-day Devotional
Wisdom for Mothers – a 30-day Devotional
Wisdom for Fathers – a 30-day Devotional
Wisdom for Work – a 30-day Devotional

JOIN OUR ONLINE COMMUNITY

SIGN UP for your free "Wisdom Hunters...Right Thinking" daily
devotional e-mail at **wisdomhunters.com**
"LIKE" us on Facebook at **facebook.com/wisdomhunters**
FOLLOW us on Twitter at **twitter.com/wisdomhunters**
SUBSCRIBE to us on YouTube at
youtube.com/wisdomhuntersvids
DOWNLOAD the free Wisdom Hunters App for
tablets and mobile devices on iTunes and Google Play

TABLE OF CONTENTS

1

Love Is Patient

I Corinthians 13:4

Love is patient. It is patient because it is more concerned with the welfare of another than its own needs. It is patient because it is more motivated to make the relationship right than to be right. Patience is the prerogative of the person who loves, so love can't help but be patient.

It is the job description of everyone who loves because patience is the fruit of people filled with the Holy Spirit. Patience comes out of your heart when love dominates it (Ephesians 4:2). When the pressure of life squeezes you, patience comes out. Like a chocolate covered cherry, there is something delicious on the inside.

Furthermore, patience stunts anger's growth by not feeding its appetite. It lovingly replaces anger with grace and forgiveness. Patience understands that most anger is destructive and self-centered, so it deflects anger by being other-centered. It looks out for the welfare of other human beings for their sake and for the purpose of being an image bearer of Christ.

When people see patience, they see the example of Jesus' attitude and behavior. He was more patient with sinners who didn't know any better than He was with religious leaders who should have known better (John 8:7).

Patience oozed out of the pores of Christ's character like a perspiring body on a sultry summer day at the beach. Patience is a priority for people who seek to love as their Savior loves. Indeed, patience is not reserved for the radically righteous, but is accessible for all who desire to love.

So, learn to love in a patient manner. The reason you are patient with your spouse is because you love him or her. The reason you are patient with people who make you uncomfortable is that you love them. There is a difference between being reluctantly tolerant and lovingly patient.

Patience begins with loving oneself, so do not despise or look down on how God has made you. If you don't love and respect yourself you will be impatient with your love and respect of others, so relax. The second greatest command: love others as you love yourself (Matthew 22:37-39).

Jesus patiently loves you just as you are. Therefore, you can love others and exercise patience in the same unconditional way Christ loves you. Patient people actively and meaningfully plan to love, so be patient on the phone with the incompetent customer representative.

Be patient with your single-parent restaurant server who is tired, afraid, and anxious. Be patient with your family member who is outside of the faith and uncomfortable with your character. You love when you are patient. Therefore, pray for patience, and you will increase your capacity to love. Be like Jesus, and be a patient lover of people.

How can I patiently love others with the patient love of the Lord?

Related Readings: Nehemiah 9:30; Proverbs 16:33; James 5:7; 2 Peter 3:9

2

Love Is Kind

I Corinthians 13:4

Kindness means you are pleasant to be around because your countenance is inviting and shows interest. It is as much an attitude as anything, and it is the ability to see beyond the immediate to the potential. Kindness means you go out of your way to love others.

People who are unlovable become prime candidates for your kindness. A family member who is far from God, deep down desires unconditional love and kindness. Kindness is a natural application of love because it makes one feel loved. It is the ability to be accepting when everything within you wants to be rejecting. It is a strategy for forgiveness when you are wronged or when someone takes advantage of you. When your trusting spirit has been violated, you still love by being kind—stop fighting, and start forgiving.

Love keeps you kind, especially toward those who are closest to you. They do not deserve you dredging up hurtful, bitter, and unforgiving words from the past. Love is kind in its conversations. Harsh and abrasive speech is absent from kind conversation. Love produces words that are "kind and tenderhearted" (Ephesians 4:32).

Love is able to extend kind words that cheer up heavy hearts (Proverbs 16:24). Pray to God for kindness to reign in your relationships with kids and teenagers. Children translate kindness into love, for it is their language of love.

The temptation is to disrespect when we have been disrespected, and the natural response is to become angry when someone else spews out his or her frustrations on us. But God has not called us to natural responses but supernatural ones.

Kindness in the face of frustration is a fruit of the Spirit, and only through submission to your Savior will kindness become front and center. The fullness of the Holy Spirit in your life is what causes kindness to come forth.

Lastly, loving others with kindness does not preclude difficult decisions. Kindness is not patronizing, but it is authentic care and concern, and it is able to deliver hard truth that softens hard hearts. You can dismiss an employee with kindness or disagree with kindness.

Harshness has no hold on those who are controlled by Christ. Therefore, kindly love people through difficult situations. Serve those who are experiencing financial difficulties, for example. Kindness is king for followers of King Jesus, so love with kindness and watch them come around and embrace Christ.

Kindness kills sin and sadness, and it brings to life love, forgiveness, and hope. Allow Jesus' loving kindness to flow through you, for kindness toward the needy honors God (Proverbs 14:31). Kindness resides where love is applied.

What hard conversation do I need to have with a kind attitude?

Related Readings: Ruth 3:20; Job 6:14; 2 Cor. 6:6; Colossians 3:12

3

Love Does Not Envy

I Corinthians 13:4

Love is not envious. It celebrates the good fortune of others and smiles when some-one succeeds because love is an envy eraser. It can't wait for someone else to reach their goals and get the attention and accolades, for it is emotionally secure and mature.

Love does not depend on the "desire to get" for contentment, because its contentment rests with Christ. It is content knowing that God "rains on the just and on the unjust" (Matthew 5:45). God's grace and blessing cannot be figured out or bottled in a formula, for He withholds or gives His blessing at His discretion.

Christ, of course, has established principles that, if obeyed, lead to blessing (Psalm 119:1-2). If you obey your parents, you will be blessed by their wisdom, experience, and love. If you follow the laws of the land, you will be free from serving a prison term or paying fines.

God's truth can be applied and benefited from by both believers and unbelievers. His ways work; so don't get worked up when the wicked succeed. Success in life is an option for anyone who implements the principles embedded in God's Word. Envy attracts the immature, the insecure, the greedy, and the faithless.

Comparison with people is an incubator for envy. Instead, reserve your comparisons for the character of Christ and be comfortable with yourself. Your personality, your looks and your gifts are from God, so be whom God created. Love is content to be God's unique creation. Envy looks at the stuff of others and salivates for the same.

Envy wants to get, while love wants to give. It wants a woman's smooth skin, a man's car, or wealth's options. Love overcomes these sometimes surreal and selfish desires by finding contentment in Christ. Thus seek affirmation from Almighty God in place of

10

the acquisition of stuff.

Love is well versed in congratulating, by making milestones into big deals. For example, completed projects, anniversaries, and birthdays are celebrated as a work team or family. Moreover, a sure remedy for envy is giving. Love gives sincere compliments, money, credit, time, and it gives the benefit of the doubt.

Love's generosity deflates envy's influence. Wish well those who have done well and be grateful to God for their good fortune. A mature man or woman is motivated to excellence by those who have achieved. Love those who succeed, and recognize their achievements. Promote your protégé or be glad for the success of your ex-spouse.

Learn from, don't loathe, your competition. Love your enemies (Luke 6:35) and pray for them, and love those who forgot you after you helped them succeed. Envy leads to a life of discontentment and sorrow, but love is Christ-centered, content, and joyful. Envy has no place for a person who lavishly loves God and people.

How can I celebrate the accomplishment of others with love and respect?

Related Readings: Proverbs 14:30; 23:17; Mark 7:21-23; James 3:14-16

4

Love Does Not Boast

I Corinthians 13:4

Love does not need to brag because those who boast seek security within themselves. Boasting is for those who need something more than eternity's endorsement. It is bad because it brings the attention down to one person instead of the team.

This is a struggle for all of us because we want our peers to admire our abilities and our accomplishments, and we want them to see us as intelligent and capable. We want to be perceived as spiritually mature and we want to have a reputation as a man or woman who loves and respects our spouse and our family.

We want to reveal our résumé and say that the reason we're in our current position is our hard work and perseverance. Our flesh lobbies for recognition. Even the most committed of Jesus' disciples struggled with taming their egos. James and John wanted to know on which side of the throne they would sit when Christ entered into His kingdom (Mark 10:37-40).

However, love learns to leave these matters in the Lord's hands by deflecting attention away from itself. It is the ability to tell a story without having to be the lead actor in the plot. Love lifts up others and lowers itself. You are able to bring out the best in people because you extend to them sincere compliments and affirmation. Love is not all about you, but all about others.

Love seeks ways to give its Savior credit for accomplishments. It is not a flippant, "Praise the Lord!" Rather, it is heartfelt humility and thankfulness. Our communication with body language and words says that without God, we fail. He answers prayer by giving us wisdom.

He grows our character and forgives our sin. He blesses us with family and friends who love Him. Love looks long and hard to the Lord, and any boasting is limited to Him.

James describes the sin of self-boasting, "As it is, you boast and brag. All such boasting is evil" (James 4:16).

Love smothers the need to brag, and it is so caught up with reaching out to others that it forgets to stick a feather in its own cap. Love wants to know what you know by understanding your passions, fears, and dreams. Bragging is all about self; love is all about others.

Ironically, boasting is totally unnecessary because the truth will eventually triumph. You do not have to tell others what they already know or will discover. Love understands this and rests, knowing that the revelation of who you are will come out over time, good or bad.

Love trusts God to elevate its standing in His timing. Boasting repels people, but love draws them inward. Therefore, invite people in with your love and lead them to the Lord. He gets the glory, and you get the incredible satisfaction of following Him. Above all else, let your love brag on Jesus. Give God glory and give people credit for your success.

How can I better brag on the Lord and people and avoid recognition?

Related Readings: Psalm 44:8; Proverbs 27:1; 2 Corinthians 12:5-9

5

Love Is Not Proud

I Corinthians 13:4

Love is not proud. Indeed, there is no room for pride in a heart of love. Pride is an anchor to love that restrains its rich offering. It prolongs the inability to love by short-circuiting the effect of agape love. Pride is a precursor to loveless living; it struggles with love because it requires a focus off itself and onto others.

Pride is deceptive, as it always negotiates for its own benefit. There is a driving force behind pride that is unhealthy and unnecessary. Moreover, it is indiscriminate in its seduction of either gender. Men may be the most susceptible to pride's illusion, but women can be deceived just as well. Eve fell into this trap in her encounter with the devil (1 Timothy 2:14).

Pride's feeling of superiority slices into the soul like a surgeon's scalpel. It inserts its influence deep and wide. You can be controlled and wired by pride and not even know it. Love longs to have the same status as power-hungry pride. Love seeks to defuse pride's time bomb of terror and coercion. Love outlasts pride if applied humbly and heavily.

Instead of demanding its own way, love seeks to make those around it successful. Love listens; pride talks. Love forgives; pride resents. Love gives; pride takes. Love apologizes; pride blames. Love understands; pride assumes. Love accepts; pride rejects. Love trusts; pride doubts. Love asks; pride tells. Love leads; pride drives.

Love frees up; pride binds up. Love builds up; pride tears down. Love encourages; pride discourages. Love confronts; pride is passive-aggressive. Love is peaceful; pride is fearful. Love clarifies with truth; pride confuses with lies. But, love comes alive with humility.

14

Most importantly, humility is a hotbed of love. It has the opposite effect on love than does pride. Humility invites love to take up permanent residence in the human heart. Love covers a multitude of sins (1 Peter 4:8), and humility understands that love is reserved for all.

Love forgives even the worst of sinners, as pride struggles in a life of bitterness and resentment, thinking somehow it is paying back the offender. This state of unresolved anger only eats up the one unable to love and forgive. Furthermore, humility positions you to love and be loved. Humility knows it needs help in receiving agape love.

Your humble heart yearns for love from your Lord Jesus Christ. Once you receive the love of your heavenly Father, you can't help but give it to others. As you receive love, you are capable of giving love.

Therefore, let the Lord love on you and allow others to love you, so you can, in turn, love. Proud hearts melt under the influence of intense and unconditional love. The calling of Christians is perpetual love; so be guilty of love. Your love is healing and inviting. Pride exits when humility enters, and then you are in a position to love.

How can I cultivate a life that loves liberally from a humble heart?

Related Readings: Psalm 31:23; 2 Timothy 3:2; Colossians 3:12

6

Love Is Not Rude

I Corinthians 13:5

Love rejects rudeness because rudeness is reserved for the insensitive and the insecure. Rudeness is impolite and disrespectful. Indeed, a rude reply stands ready on the lips of an unlovely life. Rude people use coarse words that rub their listeners the wrong way.

They pride themselves in being without airs, but they are insensitive in the timing and the tone of their conversations. They hurt feelings at the drop of a hat and seem to alienate people on purpose. However, love is the light that leads rudeness out of darkness (Romans 2:19).

A rude person is a rascal to work alongside because you never know when they are going to offend you or someone else. You lose confidence in rude people because of their volatile nature. You don't want to be embarrassed around one of their outbursts or social indiscretions, so you shun their presence. Rude people become loners by default.

Over time, no one can tolerate a barrage of irreverence and sarcasm. Even the most accepting saints grow weary of rudeness. Rudeness has no place in a caring culture. Love expunges rudeness like a healthy body does a virus. Tough love escorts rudeness out the relational door.

You need to be very direct and matter-of-fact in your communication with a rude person. Direct conversation is the only way they begin to "get it." Love takes the time to be very candid and clear with rude people who run roughshod over others. However, be careful not to be rude in dealing with the rude. Be prayed up and filled up with the Spirit before you encounter the rude with truth (Romans 9:1).

Without patronizing, love is able to find at least one thing they admire in someone else. Even if a person is full of himself, there lies dormant, within him or her, some redeeming quality. Love is able to pull out the potential for good that lies deep within a selfish soul; the way Barnabas saw possibilities in Saul (Acts 9:27).

Love looks beyond the hard, crusty exterior of someone's character and understands that fear may have locked his or her love into solitary confinement. They feel lost, lonely, and afraid. Nonetheless, love is able to get past this rude roadblock and inject faith.

Faith in God, faith in oneself, and faith in others frees one from rudeness. The Almighty's rude awakening transforms an impolite heart into one full of kindness and grace. When love has its way, rudeness runs away. Love the rude, and watch what God can do. Their sarcasm is a smoke screen that hides a lonely, loveless, and hurt heart.

Rude people are reaching out but they don't know how. Stay committed to your rude roommate, relative, parent, child, or colleague. Love them to Jesus, and your unconditional love will melt away their iceberg-like insecurities. Pray they will see themselves as Christ sees them, and pray they will love and be loved. Love loves the rude and is not rude.

What rude person needs my loving acceptance?

Related Readings: Psalm 144:3; Proverbs 29:7; Luke 4:24; John 13:20

7

Love Is Not Self-Seeking

I Corinthians 13:5

Love is not self-seeking. It seeks instead the Kingdom of God and His righteousness (Matthew 6:33). Like a heat-seeking missile, love is locked onto the warm heart of God. Self is lowered to the bottom shelf and God is elevated to the top shelf.

Love understands that it is all about Him. Its top priority is not to look out for number one, but to look to the One. Love seeks its Savior, Jesus, moment by moment, for wisdom and direction. Self seeks its own way; love seeks God's way. Self seeks praise; love seeks to praise. Self is fearful of being found out; love is an open book.

Self is self-absorbed; love is saturated in the Spirit. Self is preoccupied with pleasing people; love is compelled to follow the commands of Christ. The goal of love is self-denial and to serve others on behalf of Jesus. Love dies daily to self and comes alive for Christ.

Prayer is your expression of love for the Lord. It places your affections above self-satisfaction toward what pleases God. It is very difficult, if not impossible, to remain self-seeking when seeking the Lord in prayer, confession, and repentance (Hosea 10:12).

This self-seeking scenario also applies to our horizontal relationships with people. Love seeks to meet the needs of people first, even above its own. Love understands and is not afraid to deny self for the sake of a spouse or friend. Families provide a daily opportunity for selfless living where you can selfishly demand your way or you can lovingly serve others.

The outside world also provides similar opportunities to put others first. It is far more fulfilling to seek the welfare of widows and orphans than your own life of leisure. Use your position and influence for the good of other people by giving up and/or giving away self-seeking rewards. This is counter-intuitive and countercultural.

Someone will probably take advantage of your good will; as a consequence your unselfishness may become a chronic cross you bear. But any cross you bear is a reflection of the cross Christ bore. If it had been about His physical and emotional needs, He would not have been obedient to the cross (Hebrews 12:2-3).

Jesus' goal was to do the will of His heavenly Father (John 17:4). Jesus loved by doing God's will over His own will. He subjugated His selfish desires to eternal interests. Since Jesus trusted His heavenly Father, so can you. Your choice to love others may mean death to your own desires, but it will provide life in your relationships.

As Jesus said, "But many who are first will be last and many who are last will be first" (Matthew 19:30). Love may finish last in man's eyes, but wins the gold in God's eyes. Love seeks its Savior first, and it serves others. Love is a Savior-seeker, not a self-seeker.

How can I channel my love into seeking God's Kingdom and not my own?

Related Readings: Psalm 119:36; Proverbs 18:1; Romans 2:8; Titus 2:2

8

Love Is Not Easily Angered

I Corinthians 13:5

Love is slow to anger and it is not easily angered. It is not in a hurry to get angry because it knows God is at work. Love knows God can handle the irregular person and the stressful situation. Most of the time, the best thing love can do is refrain from anger. A calm response diffuses an angry outburst (Proverbs 15:1).

Poverty, AIDS, and terrorism should work us up much more than traffic, forgetful waiters, and not getting our way. Indeed, apply anger appropriately and proportionately to the degree of injustice to the underdog. But love overlooks the silly things that really don't matter that much in the big scheme of things.

A friend or family member who is rarely on time is no reason to get angry. Instead, adjust your expectations and build a time buffer into your schedule. Why get angry when a little bit of adjustment remedies the situation? Love adjusts rather than stews in anger; it calms the nerves, while anger wreaks havoc with your blood pressure. Love-filled living is by far a healthier way to live physically and emotionally.

Love is able to keep the big picture in mind. It understands that tomorrow is another day and there is no need to stress over this temporary setback. God will work things out in His timing, for He can be trusted. It is much wiser to trust God with your spouse, instead of attempting to whip him or her into shape with your anger.

God's discipline is much more thorough and precise. He puts His finger on an attitude or action and won't let up until He is satisfied with the resulting change. Love knows how to trust God. Therefore, pray to God before you get angry. Ask the Lord to increase your love quotient before you lash out in anger.

Love understands there are better ways and a better day ahead. However, there are times love sees the need for anger. Your love needs to rise up in anger over the abuses of drugs and alcohol. These are enemies of unsuspecting souls that wreck relationships and take lives.

Your love can confidently invite anger to rise up and rebuke these artificial enhancers of hope that logically lead to death. Love doesn't stick its head in the sand of isolation and detachment, but engages by offering wise choices and compassionate counseling.

Love is all about solutions to the seduction of sin. Love is angered by sin's control of a loved one's soul. It drives us to our knees in our own confession of sin and to our feet to be a part of the solution. Love gets angry at times, but is reserved for the right occasions.

Even Jesus administered anger at the appropriate time (Mark 3:5, John 2:15). Love will anger at times, but only after much prayer and patience. Love more and be angry less. Above all else, be rich in love and slow to anger (Psalm 145:8).

What situation or person requires me to be slow to anger and trust God?

Related Readings: Numbers 14:18; Joel 2:13; 1 Timothy 2:8; James 1:20

9

Love Keeps
No Record of Wrongs

I Corinthians 13:5

Love forgives continually and it forgives comprehensively. Forgiveness wipes clean the slate of offense, hence it is freeing for everyone. Indeed, forgiveness was the heartbeat of Jesus. Some of His last words requested forgiveness from God for the ignorant acts of His offenders.

Christ's greatest act of love was the forgiveness He extended by His voluntary death on the cross (Colossians 2:13-15). Jesus described His own act of love when He said, "Greater love has no one than this, that he lay down his life for his friends" (John 15:13).

Forgiveness is the fuel for living a life free from the clutter of cutting words or unjust acts. A life without forgiveness is a lonely life locked up in the solitary confinement of sin. Forgiveness flows when you have been authentically and thoroughly forgiven.

Half-hearted forgiveness is the destiny of those who have not tasted the tender touch of forgiveness from their heavenly Father. Unless the forgiveness of God has graced your heart and soul, your capacity for forgiveness will be foreign and futile.

It is the grace of God and faith in Him that fuels forgiveness in followers of Christ. The job description of Christians is to love with forgiveness because we have been forgiven (Colossians 3:13). Think about the depth and breadth of your forgiveness. Ignorant acts, forgiven; drunkenness, it's forgiven; lust, it's forgiven; immorality, it's forgiven; hate, it's forgiven; ignoring God, it's forgiven; unbelief, it's forgiven. Love forgives because it has been forgiven.

Remember where you were BC (before Christ), and reflect on where you would be today without His love and forgiveness. Recall what it was like to be lost and bound up in your sin, and celebrate how far God has brought you. Love is extremely grateful for God's goodness and redeeming power. Forgiveness is second nature and somewhat automatic for followers of Jesus who are consumed with Christ's love.

They are enamored with God's love for them and others. When you have been forgiven much, you love much (Luke 7:47). Your capacity to love is directly tied to your willingness to receive Christ's forgiveness. Accept the Almighty's forgiveness so you can extend forgiveness.

Love looks for excuses to eliminate hard feelings, as it replaces resentment and bitterness with love and forgiveness. Love by forgiving your family member who may not even know they hurt your heart. Love by forgiving your friend who volitionally violated your confidence.

Love by forgiving your father and mother who are preoccupied parents. Love by forgiving your child who is ungrateful and selfish. Love by forgiving yourself for your unwise decisions. Forgiveness forgets the past, engages in the present, and hopes in the future. Love forgives!

Whom do I need to love and forgive by the grace of God given to me?

Related Readings: Genesis 50:17; Numbers 14:19; 2 Corinthians 2:10

10

Love Does Not Delight In Evil

I Corinthians 13:6

Love avoids evil by not delighting in its alluring temptations. Evil is an outcast of love, and it has no room for sin in its circle of wise influences. Evil seeks to destroy love. Indeed, sin is the hatchet man for hell and it lures in both the rich and the poor.

It is relentless in its pursuit to replace love with lust. Sin takes well-meaning workers and grinds them into workaholics. It takes people under extreme pressure and turns them into alcoholics. It portrays drugs as cool, euphoric, and romantic. But love sees beyond the momentary escape, the temporary release, and the artificial high. Love longs for the authentic and the real. Love does not cohabitate with sin because it is counter to the cause of Christ.

Sin is the enemy, and love does not sleep with the enemy. Love does not flirt with sinful people or experiment with sin; it is not worth it. Not to mention that sin and evil break the heart of God. Sin may lure you in with good looks and false promises, but its outcomes are outrageously bad. There is no good that comes from a force that is the antithesis of the Almighty.

Satan will continue to unleash his evil strategies until our Savior returns the second time. Then, after a period of time, the devil and his evil endeavors will be cast into the lake of fire forever (Revelation 20:10). But for now, the role of love is to reject any demonic evil advances.

Jesus Christ is the focus and attraction for those motivated by love. Faith is not lukewarm for men or women who love God, for they fear becoming distasteful to their Savior (Revelation 3:16). Without hot and committed love, you are disqualified to engage in Kingdom initiatives. Furthermore, love does not perceive church attendance as a perfunctory exercise done out of obligation or guilt.

Love sees the church as the "Bride of Christ," so it is not cold or dispassionate toward Christ or His church. Committed disciples of Christ cannot straddle the fence with one foot flirting with sin and the other with evil. Love is an either/or proposition, not a both/and one. You are either for Him or against Him (Luke 11:23).

The passion of Jesus-followers is to love and obey God. When your focus is on Him, there is no room for evil. The agenda of love is to delight in the Lord; it is preoccupied with pleasing God. Love can't wait to commune with Christ because its desire is intimacy with Almighty God.

Love flushes out evil desires and sinful thoughts as it loves and obeys God. Love has no time for sin because it is caught up with Christ. Therefore, stay away from sin, run from evil, and run toward God. Disengage from people who lean toward evil. Be true to the One who loves you most. At the cross His love overcame evil, so express your love by delighting in Jesus.

What are some ways I can delight in the Lord with my faith and family?

Related Readings: Psalm 119:47; Zephaniah 3:17; Matthew 12:18

11

Love Rejoices with the Truth

I Corinthians 13:6

Since love enjoys truth, it seeks it out and rejoices in the ramifications of its application. Love knows truth comes from the Father, and it is His way to lead and direct you in His will. Truth is a tremendous asset to love because it illuminates the way.

Truth teaches love where to apply itself, and love teaches truth how to apply itself. Truth delivered in love brings joy; it brings a smile to the face of love. Love is pleased to give and receive the truth. However, love without truth is shallow and sentimental because it has no lasting effect. Truth without love is harsh and abrasive and is rarely received well. Love and truth need each other.

Jesus modeled this when He lovingly spoke to both the woman caught in adultery and to her accusers. He confronted the sin of both parties with a spirit of redemption and love (John 8:3-11). Indeed, love uses the truth as a facilitator of faith and obedience to God.

It can't wait to understand and apply truth, because it knows its positive outcomes. Love knows that truth is a tool of the Lord by which He grows you up in Him, and it gets excited over the possibilities of becoming more like Jesus. Truth has this effect on the character of Christ's followers and is the remedy for ignorance.

For example, truth reveals disrespectful attitudes in wives and replaces them with respect. Truth exposes husbands who lack love and invites them to confession and repentance. Moreover, love takes the time to speak the truth in love (Ephesians 4:15).

Many times, you can most effectively deliver truth with questions. Help people discover truth without telling them what to do. Love understands this process of honoring others by facilitating the understanding and the application of truth. Questions like, "What do you think you need to do?" "Do you really want to do this?"

"Why do you want to do this?" "Have you prayed through this?" "What does God think?" "What do your spouse and friends think?" Love loves questions because they help sincere seekers get to the essence of truth through their own self-discovery.

God used a question from the very beginning when He inquired of Adam as to his whereabouts in the garden (Genesis 3:9). God knew the answer, but He wanted Adam to think through his curious condition. God loved and respected Adam so much that He gave him the opportunity to reason and reflect on truth.

Love leads others into truth because it is a patient lover of truth. Love longs for truth to be exposed and embraced. This is what it means to love God with your mind (Matthew 22:37-39). Therefore, love truth and lovingly speak the truth. Love knows Jesus intimately, for He is Truth (John 14:6).

What truth do I need to embrace and celebrate for Christ's sake?

Related Readings: Zechariah 8:19; 2 Thessalonians 2:10; 1 Peter 1:22

12

Love Always Protects

I Corinthians 13:7

Love always protects. It protects because it loves, and it loves because it protects. Love protects physically; if you love someone, you do not want him or her to suffer bodily harm. You provide for them an environment that protects them from the elements.

You shield them from harmful substances that might damage their bodies. You keep them safe by obeying the speed limit and not driving recklessly. You protect them by not endangering their lives with unnecessary risks. If you love someone, you protect them.

Wives love to be protected; it makes them feel valued and cherished. They yearn for physical, financial, and emotional protection. Husbands, when you keep your wife safe and sound you speak their love language. Your provision of a dependable automobile and a secure home screams love.

Because you love your family, you protect them from unwise financial exposure. For example, you don't "bet the farm" and place your house at risk. Your temperament might be able to handle high risk, and even thrive on it, but because you love your family, you do not personally expose them to on-the-edge endeavors.

You do not want them to fear being unprotected within an unstable home environment. Love protects emotionally because it understands the sensitive nature of others. Emotional protection allows children to grow up well-adjusted and loved. Adolescents are vulnerable and tender; they need the loving protection of their parents.

Love prays for the protection of the ones it loves. Pray for their hearts to be protected from the evil one (2 Thessalonians 3:3) and from unwise influences. Pray for the testimony of those you love to remain unsoiled and fresh in their walk with Christ. Pray for the Holy Spirit to protect well-meaning loved ones from straying away from God's best in relationships.

Furthermore, pray for protection from yourself. If not careful, you can talk yourself into almost anything. Sometimes, you can become your own worst enemy, so pray for protection from yourself, and be accountable.

Lastly, think of ways to protect your friends and work associates. Your wisdom and counsel provide loving protection (Proverbs 4:6). A small, encouraging word may protect peers from over-commitment. Your colleagues may need your permission to say no, just so they can let go.

Do not underestimate your actions, for what you do provides protection. Your model of appropriate behavior with the opposite sex protects you and provides an example of discretion for those you influence (Proverbs 2:11). You love others by creating an environment of protection. Thus, pray for God's protection and provide protection. Love always protects.

How can I lovingly protect others and myself from unwise decisions?

Related Readings: Deuteronomy 23:14; Psalm 5:11; 25:21; John 17:11-15

13

Love Always Trusts

I Corinthians 13:7

Love always trusts, for trust is a staple of love. If you are always suspicious and uncertain, then love is lacking. Love thrives in an environment of trust, but shrivels up in a spirit of distrust. It is very difficult to love without trust, for it is a lubricant for love.

It calls out love like an engagement invitation. Trust is what it takes for a love relationship to flourish and take root. Therefore, look for the best in someone else and trust them, even though they may not have been trustworthy in the past. Love is all about second chances. Of course, you must be responsible as a good steward of money and time.

Don't blindly believe everything everyone tells you. Have instead a policy of "trust and verify." On the other hand, love does not write someone off when they fail to meet expectations, or when they blatantly experience failure. Love picks them up and says, "I will trust you again," "I have not given up on you," "You are on the team," "You are a child of God, therefore you deserve another opportunity to succeed."

Love is all about making people successful. When you love someone, you trust them to carry out the plan. Love sees trust where others see distrust. Love sees potential where others see disqualification. Love sees success where others see failure. Love sees a hurting human being where others see someone who is just angry.

Love thinks the best, but distrust thinks the worst. Love and trust feed off each other; they propel one another to greater heights. Love always trusts. This is especially true with Almighty God. Love trusts God, for He is trustworthy. His track record of trustworthiness is without blemish. He can be trusted. If you love Him, you will trust Him. Your affection and love are meant to originate in heaven not on earth. Love leans on and listens to the Lord because it trusts Him.

So the goal is to fall more deeply in love with God. Go deeper with God, and you will become more and more infatuated with Him and His ways. John explains it well: "And so we know and rely on the love God has for us. God is love. Whoever lives in love lives in God, and God in him" (I John 4:16).

Indeed, His love relationship is based on trust. God is your lover. He is a lover of your mind, soul, body, and emotions. You can trust Him to love you authentically and unconditionally. He has no inhibitions in His love toward you, for His intimacy is uninhibited. Therefore, you love better when you regularly receive the love of God.

Because He loves you, you love better, and because you love, you trust. Sad is the soul that has not learned the secret of loving by trusting. The conditional lover is always looking over their shoulder in distrust. Cynicism creates a cold heart. However, your heavenly Father wants to flood your heart with love. Your trust in God accelerates in direct proportion to your intimacy with Jesus. Love always trusts.

Does my love and trust in others flow out of my love and trust in God?

Related Readings: Psalm 9:10; 26:1; John 14:15-17; Romans 15:13

14

Appointments for Love

Let us go early to the vineyards to see if the vines have budded, if their blossoms have opened, and if the pomegranates are in bloom—there I will give you my love.
Song of Songs 7:12

Many things compete with your marriage. Work, children, parents, money, hobbies, friends, volunteerism, selfish desires and life in general can masquerade as marriage competitors. So, how can you transform these competitors to your marriage, into compliments to your marriage?

First, when you make marriage a priority, the other important things that clamor for your attention become secondary and supportive. This is wisdom, because marriage is not meant to get the leftovers of your life, for its vitality will melt in the face of neglect. Yet, if you are intentional in your marriage appointments, it will flourish with freshness. It's a priority when it is embraced by your calendar.

Husbands and wives need focused quantity time with each other, because quality time flows out of quantity time. Quality time is a consequence of an environment with the least distractions. Cell phones are silenced and there is a cease-fire from interruptions. 'Fast' from e-mail, so there can be a focus on friendship.

Co-existing does not create intimacy in marriage, but intentionality to get to know one another deeply does. Romance is the result of regular real time together in communication, care and understanding. Indeed, physical intimacy between husband and wife is part of God's game plan (I Corinthians 7:3-5).

Therefore, make routine appointments to love your spouse. Pull out your calendars and create a time just for the two of you. The best gift you give to your children, next to faith in God, is a healthy marriage. So, make appointments for emotional love and physical love.

Emotional love may be unfiltered listening and learning about the fears and fantasies of the other. Make your spouse feel secure by being trustworthy and respectful, and listen intently to their struggles and disappointments. Secondly, fatigue and busyness are twin tyrants looming over physical love.

However, you can dethrone these detractors with focused time for a husband's release and a wife's fulfillment. Romance one another with a date night, by dressing up and smelling good, as if it were a grand occasion. Woo each other with the fire and excitement of youth. Adultery is not even an after thought in an enthusiastic love life.

Yes, physical intimacy needs to be planned and prepared for, and let any spontaneous rendezvous be a bonus. Make sure to calendar time where you have an occasional overnight together, or a week of vacation for just the two of you. Use the calendar to create emotional and physical intimacy. The Bible teaches there is a time for everything, even a time to love (Ecclesiastes 3:8). Make appointments for love and love!

When can we set our next appointment for love? Ongoing appointments?

Related Readings: Ruth 4:10-11; 1 Corinthians 9:5; 1 Timothy 3:12

15

Love Always Hopes

I Corinthians 13:7

Love always hopes. It hopes for the best and is prepared for the worst. It is hopeful because its hope is in the Lord. As the old hymn proclaims, "My hope is built on nothing less than Jesus' blood and righteousness." When we love God, we also hope in Him because we are sure of His promises that transcend hope and provide assurance.

Promises such as, "Never will I leave you; never will I forsake you" (Hebrews 13:5b). Moreover, faith helps us be sure of what we hope for. As it says in Hebrews 11:1: "Now faith is being sure of what we hope for and certain of what we do not see." Faith, hope, and love are all first cousins; they complement each other and support one another.

Love hopes because it knows the end of the story, for heaven is its destiny. It bridles its emotions to not fear because love casts out fear (I John 4:18, NKJV). Hope conquers death and fear because Jesus has gone before us and done the same (Acts 2:23-24).

Therefore, you can be hopeful because you get to hang out in heaven with your Lord and Savior, Jesus. But there is something just as big that you can hope for in real time. You can hope that others you love will place their faith in Jesus Christ.

You know it is God's will for them to be saved from their sin (2 Peter 3:9), but your part is not to get them saved, but to love them to the Lord. Some plant and some water, but it is God who makes faith grow (1 Corinthians 3:6). It is the Lord who convicts and draws people unto Himself. But be hopeful. If God can save us, He can save anybody.

Love always hopes, especially when you are drowning in adversity. You may feel like you can only come up for air one more time. The undertow of your circumstances may be sucking you out into the sea of despair. Your emotional energy may be overspent and close to bankruptcy.

Your marriage seems hopeless, but you are still called to love. Your health has ravaged hope, but you are still called to love. A relationship may be hopeless, but you are still called to love. Your finances are struggling to be hopeful, but you are still called to love.

Hopelessness has hijacked your work, but God still calls you to love. Love in spite of your sorry situation, and the feelings of hope will catch up. You do not have to love the situation, but you can still love those around you. You can love the Lord, and you can love yourself.

It is okay to not like what you are going through right now, but continue to love. Love, for love leads to hope and drops despair. Hope follows love as ducklings follow their mother. Love is a creator of hope. Therefore, anticipate the outcomes of aligning with Almighty God's agenda. Love Him and love others. Love especially when you don't feel like loving. Be hopeful, for love always hopes.

How can I express a hopeful love to hurting and hopeless relationships?

Related Readings: Psalm 33:22; 130:7; Romans 5:5; Colossians 1:5

16

Love Always Perseveres

I Corinthians 13:7

Love always perseveres. It does not give up. This is why the love commitment of husbands and wives is "till death do us part." This is the assurance that accompanies love, for it is loyal in the face of hard times. "I don't love you anymore" is not an option for couples committed to Christ. Love always perseveres.

It perseveres through problems; it perseveres through misunderstandings; it perseveres though uncertainty; it perseveres through unfair arguments; it perseveres through persecution, divorce, and abandonment; it perseveres through a lawsuit or being fired.

Love becomes better instead of bitter when experiencing a raw deal. God's grace and love provide you the lasting ability for extraordinary love. Indeed, if your heavenly Father didn't personally love you, your love would be lethargic.

It would be sluggish in its application to others if you were not daily loved by the Lord. You can't be an unconditional lover if you don't receive the unconditional love of Jesus. Therefore, love always perseveres in the process of being loved and extending love.

This is why a parent perseveres in his or her love for their child. They can only give up on loving their loved one when their heavenly Father gives up on loving them. Parents persevere with their children because they love their children.

Even through the hurt, rejection, selfishness, financial irresponsibility, and anger, love still stands. Love will not stand down to the devil's strongholds in a young person's mind and heart. Remind your children truth and their identity is in Christ.

Your child is forgiven by you and by God; remind them of this. God has uniquely gifted your child; remind them of this. Love perseveres in reminding and revealing truth to those it loves. Pray the eyes of your child's heart will see and understand the truth of who they are from God's perspective. They long to be loved, so love them unconditionally.

Lastly, persevere in your love for your parents. Parents can be distant and disinterested, but still love them. To some degree, they may still be licking the wounds of past hurts and disappointments. Love your mom and dad while they are still alive.

One day they will not be around to love, so express all your love for your parents in this life. You plan for no regrets when you aggressively love them now. They may have chronically hurt you, but still love them. They may not love back, but still love them.

Above all, you may need to rest in, receive, and be rejuvenated by the loving relationship of your friend, Jesus. Slow down and be loved. Persevere in your love, and one day you will be grateful you did.

Who is hard to love that needs my persevering love?

Related Readings: 2 Samuel 1:23; Hebrews 11:27; Revelation 2:2-4

17

Love Never Fails

I Corinthians 13:8

Because you are successful when you love, love never fails. Failure is not an option for love because you can only succeed. With love, success is guaranteed, though it may seem like you are losing when love is not getting the desired results. You can labor in love with someone for a long period of time, and they still seem unfazed by your unconditional "agape."

However, you are still successful; you get an A for your consistent efforts to love. Some may describe your scenario as unsuccessful, but you know better. You know that if you have been obedient to love, the results are in God's hands (Deuteronomy 30:16). He is the one who can soften a hardened heart, and He is the one who can change a person's mind. Love never fails because Almighty God is its author.

Your part is to love and His part is to draw people to Himself (Jeremiah 31:3). Love in your leadership, and you are successful; love in your marriage, and you are success-ful; love in your friendships, and you are successful; love in your speech and behavior, and you are a roaring success.

Unfortunately, a person can have a rich net worth but character that lacks love. If they fail to love, they fail. Furthermore, your increase in resources provides a variety of options by which to express your love. Make it one of your goals to be as successful in your loving as you are in your business or career.

"Now that you have purified yourselves by obeying the truth so that you have sincere love for your brothers, love one another deeply, from the heart" (1 Peter 1:22).

This is why moms are celebrities of love; they love long and they love hard. Moms are unselfish lovers because they love when no one is looking. In the middle of the night, they minister to their little ones. Your motherly love is a badge of honor. Moms are the unsung heroes of unselfish love.

You may feel like a failure with your children because parenting is hard. It is hard to teach, train, and lead your children to obey God, and sometimes it is hard to love them. You want to pull out the hair from their sweet little scalps, instead of planting a loving kiss on their fragile foreheads. And because you never stop loving them, you do not fail. You are successful when you love by imparting wisdom (Proverbs 4:6).

Indeed, there are lots of ways you can fail. You can fail in your job; you can fail in your finances; you can fail in school; you can fail to follow up. But, you can never fail when you love. It may mean resigning from a time-consuming responsibility so that you have more margin for love. Heaven gives you high marks for your unconditional love, so stay enrolled in the school of love, and graduate when you get to glory.

What are some ways I can celebrate God's successes of love through me?

Related Readings: Psalm 77:8; 89:28; Lamentations 3:22

18

Love is the Greatest

I Corinthians 13:13

Why is love the greatest out of three worthy contenders? It is the greatest because it is God, for He is love (1 John 4:8). The apex of God's attributes is love. This is why you go to God first for love. He is the lover of your soul, and the love of God far exceeds earth's limited love.

This is the reason you look to Jesus as the supreme example of how to love. He says the two greatest commands hinge on love (Matthew 22:37-39). Love is God's gold standard; it rises above other compelling character traits such as faith and hope.

Love is the theme that covers your character, seasons your service for Christ, and flavors your faith. It gives off a sweet aroma through trust, and gives gusto to grace. Love adds hotness to hope, potency to patience, and spice to selflessness. It brings brilliant Technicolor to life, in contrast to our bland black-and-white loveless living.

You can serve, provide for your families, cook a meal, feed the poor, attend church, and even worship; but if these lack love, you lose. You lose the blessing of God and you lose heaven's reward because your motivation was not for your Master, Jesus Christ. Love is the greatest because it aligns your heart with Almighty God and is not lacking.

You are the greatest when you love because it draws attention to Jesus. Hands down, heaven is happiest over your unconditional and relentless love. So meditate on love as you rise in the morning, work during the day, and eat dinner at night with your family. Your spouse longs to be loved; this is their greatest need from you.

So love them lavishly in ways they want to be loved. Think often on love, and your actions will begin to follow your thoughts. What drives you? Is it love? Make love your motivation, and your happiness will spill over on to others. Love jump-starts joy and prolongs peace; it decreases pride and increases humility.

Love long and hard, love unbiased and unencumbered, love early and love late. Love the rich, the poor, and everyone in between. Love during the good times and the bad. Love the deserving and undeserving. Linger long in your love, and you will be a lasting influence for the Lord.

Lastly, great love takes on different forms. Your situation may require tough love, full of accountability and action. Or your friend may be crying out for tender love, rich in encouragement and lots of listening. Pray for God's wisdom and discernment on how to love.

Your greatest contribution to mankind is love on behalf of the Lord Jesus Christ. Your greatest gift to God and others is love. Because He loved you first, you can love (I John 4:19). God is great, and He makes you great with love. You are your greatest when you get and give love.

Do I allow my heavenly Father to love me, so I in turn can love others?

Related Readings: Psalm 57:10; 69:13; Luke 7:47; 1 Corinthians 12:31

19

Honor Marriage

Marriage should be honored by all, and the marriage bed kept pure,
for God will judge the adulterer and all the sexual.. immoral.
Hebrews 13:4

Marriage is a sacred institution of God, and it is not to be taken lightly or treated with disrespect. It is easier in most cases to get a marriage license than a driver's license, but this does not give you a license to live a reckless marriage.

To honor marriage means there is an understanding of commitment and a preparation for its success. Marriage requires much more than love. It is not just a convenient way for sex and it doesn't threaten divorce when things get hard. Marriage is a lifetime of dedication to one person. Just as Jesus is committed to His bride, the church, for eternity (Revelation 19:7), so you remain faithful to your spouse.

Moreover, keep your marriage bed pure. You honor marriage when you keep the Lord's definition—a man and a woman exclusively devoted and in love with each other—under the submission of Almighty God. Do not chase after a fantasy of sexual perfection with someone other than your spouse. Sex outside of marriage is wrong, and it breaks the heart of God and crushes the spirit of your spouse.

It is not a casual infraction, for its effects last a lifetime. However, leave it to God and a scriptural process on how and when to judge the adulterer. Hold back your rocks of verbal assault and forgive (John 8:3-11). Most importantly, prevent unfaithfulness by keeping your marriage bed pure and honorable and by falling deeper and deeper in love with the man or woman God has given you.

Lastly, create boundaries together, such as committing to one another that divorce is not an option. This fidelity to your mate starves fear, intimidation, and manipulation. Furthermore, agree to never be alone with someone of the opposite sex. This is a way to honor each other and to not find yourselves in compromising situations.

At the very least, you will avoid the appearance of evil. A marriage discipline of fidelity takes effort, definition, and accountability. Yes, you trust your wife or husband, but do not be naïve to think that temptation, Satan, and other lonely souls are not out to snare your spouse (Proverbs 7:10-23). Be on the offensive by planning purity.

One way to plan purity is to honor your spouse with your words. Words of disappointment and dissatisfaction about your spouse—shared indiscreetly with the opposite sex—fuel the fires of unfaithfulness. Unfaithfulness starts with words, is furthered by indiscretion, and is executed by actions facilitated over a meal or a walk with a "friend."

Therefore, remain true to your marriage vows and your marriage mate by exercising love and respect. Be smart, and create a robust love life, for a satisfying sex life at home is a strong preventative to adultery outside the home. Above all, honor your marriage by first honoring God.

How can I honor my marriage in a way that honors the Lord?

Related Readings: 1 Corinthians 7:2; 1 Timothy 3:2; 1 Peter 3:7

20

Successful Marriages

For this reason a man will leave his father and mother and be united to his wife,
and the two will become one flesh.
Ephesians 5:31

Even successful marriages are fraught with mistakes. Marriage lessons are learned by trial and error or trial and terror, as some husbands and wives have experienced. Successful marriages don't just happen by chance—not like a clock, that's wound up and never given attention.

You become one flesh in marriage, but in reality it takes a lifetime of hard work, forgiveness, love, and respect to enjoy oneness. One flesh implies unity of purpose. It is alignment around beliefs and behavior, and if this is void in marriage, you become vulnerable to misplaced expectations and perpetual misery. Marriage requires working together.

Hard work is a necessity for successful marriages. This seems obvious, but we tend to drift toward being spousal sluggards when we become intoxicated by apathy. However, hard work is the fuel that keeps a marriage moving forward. We see the fruit of hard work in our career and raising children, as it produces satisfaction and significance.

But these results come from many hours of planning, communicating, training, and teaching. Indeed, your marriage is a direct result of the amount of effort you have expended. Don't expect a harvest of marriage success if the seeds of forgiveness, love, and respect have not been planted in the soil of humility and trust.

Furthermore, the weeds of busyness have to be intentionally pulled out, before they choke out your love and friendship with your spouse. Busyness is the enemy of the best marriages, so labor toward a marriage with much margin. Robust marriages take time and trust.

Forgiveness in marriage means you take the time to say, "I was wrong" and "I am sorry," and it means you take responsibility to confess your anger and selfishness.

Moreover, it is the ability to not hold a grudge. God-like forgiveness forgives even before the offense has been committed (Colossians 3:13). It accepts apologies and does not bring up past hurts as a club of resentment.

Forgiveness is the footers in the foundation of a successful marriage. Above all else, successful marriages are made up of unconditional love and radical respect. No wife has ever complained of too much love, or a husband of an over-abundance of respect. Love is emotional, physical, and volitional. Husbands, you are to love sensitively, intimately, and willfully (Ephesians 5:25).

Wives, respect your husband out of love and loyalty. Respect is devoid of fear, so you trust your husband because he is accountable to God. Furthermore, marriage is your laboratory for Christianity because you learn to live for the Lord by learning to live for each other. You die to yourselves and come alive to each other. Marriage is your mirror of obedience to Jesus. Successful marriages reflect your oneness with God.

What types of success does the Lord want me to experience in marriage?

Related Readings: Song of Solomon 1:15-16; 1 Cor. 7:3; Ephesians 5:33

21

Praying Husband

Isaac prayed to the LORD on behalf of his wife, because she was barren.
The LORD answered his prayer, and his wife Rebekah became pregnant.
Genesis 25:21

A praying husband appeals to the Lord for the sake of his wife. He bombards heaven on behalf of his bride with big things like having babies, and he is consistent in praying for his wife everyday for important matters such as peace and security.

Prayer is one of God's select weapons that a husband can wield in defense of his woman. God has called you to be the spiritual warrior of your home, and prayer is your first line of defense. If prayer is compromised, then you have no air support from your heavenly Father.

Without prayer covering your home and wife, you and your family are open to blistering assaults from the devil and his demons. So pray for God's hedge of protection (Job 1:10). The strategy of the stealth enemy is to keep you busy with only a token of prayer on your breath.

An overly active man is probably a prayerless man; a man consumed with his own deal is probably a prayerless man; a man absorbed by pride is probably a prayerless man; a man who serves a small God is probably a prayerless man; a man angry at his wife is probably a prayerless man. He is powerless as the spiritual leader (1 Peter 3:7).

Prayer for your wife leads you to forgive your wife, prayer for your wife leads you to love your wife, and prayer for your wife leads to the abundant life. You cannot pray for your wife and stay mad at her. You cannot pray for your wife and not want to hang out with her, for prayer facilitates intimacy. Prayer changes your heart and hers.

Therefore, agree together for a time apart just to pray (1 Corinthians 7:5), for prayer unleashes the resources and the blessings of God. Satan shudders at the thought of a praying husband. A husband will win the battle for his family if he fights the enemy on his knees. It is a posture of desperation for God that brings victory and reconciliation.

Therefore, get on your knees and do not get up until you have persevered in prayer for your helpmate. Courageously cry out to God on her behalf. Pray for her inner beauty to be reflected in her gorgeous countenance. Pray for her to feel God's love and security. Pray for her to feel your love, support, and respect.

Pray for her to be at peace with God, herself, and you. Pray for her to forgive herself and to love herself. Pray for her to have wisdom and discernment as a wife and a mom. Pray for her to love God and hate sin. As you pray, see her as God's daughter, she is forgiven and loved.

Thank the Lord for your wife and thank Him for her love for you. Thank Him for her unselfish service. Thank Him that she puts up with your idiosyncrasies. Pray for your wife that she will receive spiritual nourishment from God's Word and spiritual leadership from you.

Do I pray for my wife to be loved and protected by her heavenly Father?

Related Readings: Genesis 20:17; Luke 1:13; Ephesians 1:15-19a; 3:14-19

22

Parental Gift

Marry and have sons and daughters; find wives for your sons and give your
daughters in marriage, so that they too may have sons and daughters.
Increase in number there; do not decrease.
Jeremiah 29:6

For a parent, it is hard to give away a child in marriage. In marriage, you do gain a son
or daughter, but you still feel like you are losing something. For some parents, it is
much easier to give away time and money than to give away a child in marriage.

Even when you know in your heart it is absolutely God's will, it is still difficult. However,
this is another opportunity to point you back to God, for His timing is impeccable. It
may still be hard to accept that marriage for your child is imminent. You may reflect,
"This soon-to-be married adult child can't already be ready for marriage."

You were there for their first step, their first day of school, their first sleepover, their
first sickness, their first school play, their first athletic event, their first date, and hope-
fully, by God's grace, their first and only marriage.

It is hard to entrust your baby to someone whom you have known for only a minimal
amount of time. Even if this new in-law loves God, it is still difficult. You know in your
heart this person is the one, and you know they are meant for each other.

You know their character and maturity is robust and real. This is the right relationship,
in the right way, for the right time. It is right. Now as the parent, you have to loosen your
grip and let go. This is similar to the process you have gone through in each of your
child's transitions through life. During the good or bad stages, you held them with an
open hand and trusted God with their lives.

This is a transition of trust for you as you let them leave so they can cleave. (Mark
10:7). But, God can be trusted with your adult child, as you have trusted Him in all
other areas of your life. Your child is not exempt from this total trust. He will do a much
better job of watching over them than you ever could with your limited time and
wisdom.

His influence is far-reaching, and its expanse is much broader and deeper than a parent ripe with the truest of character. This is the role of our heavenly Father; He takes care of your children because they are His children. It is reassuring to know you parent under God's authority to pull off this impossible task of parenting.

The Lord is an expert in managing the process of your children leaving and cleaving. Your part is to pray and be a good parent. God's will is on display through this Christ-ordained marriage, for He has orchestrated a beautiful symphony of lives. Their harmony of love is uplifting and inspiring. As parents, you have done well and you can be proud. You have gained a son or daughter, and your heavenly Father is smiling and well pleased (Matthew 3:17).

Do I hold my married child with an open hand and entrust them to God?

Related Readings: Numbers 14:18; Malachi 4:6; Luke 1:17; 18:29-30

23

Ties that Bind

I led them with cords of human kindness, with ties of love;
I lifted the yoke from their neck and bent down to feed them.
Hosea 11:4

You were not created to bear your burdens alone. God is there to come alongside you and lift your burdens with His love and kindness. Burdens borne alone will break your spirit and crush your confidence. It is the compassion of Christ that lifts you to new levels of love and assurance.

Do not hide your burdens in the depths of your dark side, for if you stuff hurt into the back of your mind it will slowly seep back out in unhealthy behaviors. Praise your Savior for He daily bears your burdens (Psalm 68:19). Someone may have let you down in a big way, because you loved them much, and they have disappointed you greatly.

You love large, but they rarely reciprocate back with the same degree of love and kindness. This subtle, and sometimes not so subtle, rejection has grown into a 'big time' burden. You tried to ignore its effect on your heart, but, over time, your heart has become calloused.

Ironically, you are becoming like the one who has inflicted the harm. This burden of hurt will crush you if you do not come to terms with its raw reality. Service for your Savior and busyness in Kingdom activities will not erase its effect.

This is first and foremost between you and your heavenly Father. Go to Him and lay your burdens at His feet. Allow Him to tie up and bind your broken heart with His kindness, love, and forgiveness. He alone can bear this burden.

Manna from heaven is full of nourishment for your soul. His word is warm bread for your mind's diet. His answered prayers are cool, refreshing living water that results in mature faith and garners hope for your heart. Let the Lord nourish your needy self with eternal nutrients. He will nurse your hurt heart back to health (Matthew 13:15).

A healthy heart, made whole by its Maker, is in a position of strength to do the same for friends. He bears your burden, so you can be a burden bearer for another (Galatians 6:2). Make it a point to ask others about their tears and trials.

Your kindness and love can be the tie that binds someone's sick condition of despair into one of hope and encouragement. Look for a way to bear a brother or sister's burden in prayer, for it positions you to leverage kindness and love on behalf of the Lord.

Be a channel of Christ's love and kindness by saying a simple prayer. The Holy Spirit is the glue of grace, so pray for His regular filling. Share your burdens with your heavenly Father, and those you can trust. Then bear the burdens of other people in the faith. These are the ties that bind and they lift you to love and be loved by God and others!

Am I appropriating the Lord's love for my pain and the pain of others?

Related Readings: Psalm 32:10; Romans 8:35-39, 15:30; 2 Cor. 5:14

24

Quiet Love

The Lord your God is with you, . e is mighty to save. He will take great delight in you,
He will quiet you with his love, He will rejoice over you with singing.
Zephaniah 3:17

The love of God quiets the soul. There is nothing more soothing to the soul of a man or a woman than the love of their Savior. His love transcends the 'trash talk' of troubled people. The world's remedies can be loud and obnoxious, but not the Lord's love.

His love penetrates the proudest of hearts with gentle promptings of care and concern. Pride likes to figure things out without assistance from the love of the Lord for it sees the receiving of love as a sign of weakness. It rightly concludes that to be loved means you are dependent on something other than yourself for direction and purpose.

But, the love of God provides purpose for every recipient. Quietly and effectively God's love calms your nerves and reminds you of whose you are. You are important because you are His. You are the object of God's quiet and lavish love, for He only loves whom He values.

Love covers a multitude of sins and sorrows, "above all, love each other deeply, because love covers over a multitude of sins" (I Peter 4:8). If you are stressed, let Him quiet you with His love. If you are fearful, let Him quiet you with His love.

If you are angry, let Him quiet you with His love. If you are rejected, let Him quiet you with His love. If you are confused, let Him quiet you with His love. If you are desperate, let Him quiet you with His love. His love is active and effective.

It is not a lost love waiting to be found. His love initiates and it is seeking to find you and love you at your point of need. The love of the Lord is calling out for you, like a mom who stands at her front door calling her children to come in from play.

Don't get so busy playing and/or working that you miss God's invitation to love. Don't be so worried about work that you ignore the Lover of your soul. His love lingers over your life waiting to invade, so welcome His intimacy. God is with you and He is mighty to save.

He delights in you and desires His very best on your behalf, so be quiet and listen. Do you hear his compassionate voice? Do you feel His calming presence? His warm embrace may squeeze a tear from your eye; for this is what His love does, it moves your emotions.

He loves you simply because you are His. He cannot 'not' love you, so be still and be loved by the Lord! "The LORD appeared to us in the past, saying: "I have loved you with an everlasting love; I have drawn you with unfailing kindness" (Jeremiah 31:3).

Have I allowed the Lord's quiet love to save and soothe my soul?

Related Readings: Psalm 89:1, 103:17; Ephesians 3:18; 1 John 4:11-21

25

Meaningful Marriage

"Haven't you read," he replied, "that at the beginning the Creator 'made them male and female,' and said, 'For this reason a man will leave his father and mother and be united to his wife, and the two will become one flesh'? So they are no longer two, but one flesh. Therefore what God has joined together, let no one separate."
Matthew 19:4-6

Marriage means something, because God says it means something. He invented marriage and as the inventor is very proud of His creation. The Lord's primary purpose of a man and a woman coming together in Holy matrimony is to glorify Him. Thus a marriage built on Christ points people to His character and to His perspective on relationships.

For example God's definition of love is active and other centered, so when we read "love is kind" (1 Corinthians 13:4), we express a kind and caring attitude toward our spouse. There is a culture of humility in meaningful marriages that is quick to put the other person's needs before our own. A fulfilling marriage first follows Christ's commands.

"It does not dishonor others, it is not self-seeking, it is not easily angered, it keeps no record of wrongs" (1 Corinthians 13:5). Love looks for ways to love like God loves.

Moreover, a meaningful marriage is made up of a man and a woman who are intentional in their investment in each other. A husband cherishes his wife when he prays for her to grow in God's grace and when he seeks her counsel and advice. A wife honors her husband when she prays for him to grow in God's wisdom and when she sees him as the spiritual leader. A marriage of significance is one that plans and prepares on purpose.

"But the plans of the LORD stand firm forever, the purposes of his heart through all generations" (Psalm 33:11).

Wise are the woman and man who learn and discern the Lord's purpose for marriage and then plan to live it out. So, with bold humility hitch your marriage wagon to heaven's tractor of trust. The ride is not always smooth and easy, but it is a great adventure with Jesus and your best friend. Ride out the rough spots by faith and forgiveness—and celebrate God's goodness along the way. A meaningful marriage is fun and fulfilling for Christ's sake.

"It always protects, always trusts, always hopes, always perseveres. Love never fails" (1 Corinthians 13:7-8).

How can I make my marriage more meaningful? Have I surrendered to Christ's Lordship?

Related Readings: Joshua 15:16-17; Nehemiah 13:26; Ephesians 5:33; Philippians 2:13

26

Love Him

Love the LORD, all his saints! The LORD preserves the faithful,
but the proud he pays back in full.
Psalm 31:23

God commands His saints to love Him, and He loves you so you can love Him. Love and the Lord go hand-in-hand, for you are locked into a love relationship with your Savior. The question is not 'if' you love the Lord, but 'how' you love the Lord.

Yes your love for Christ pales in comparison to His love for you. However, you love because the Lord is worthy of your love. He longs for your love, and He invites and desires your love. Indeed, God is honored and worshiped when His saints love him. Your love holds Him in eternal esteem. What joy, for you can love the Lover of your soul.

Unredeemed sinners cannot love the Lord because they are incapable of loving Him. This is a perk that only disciples of Christ can enjoy. Unless you have been converted by the free grace of God, you cannot love Him. Love for the Lord is not unlocked until you turn the key of faith. It affords you the opportunity to love the Lord. You will remain unfulfilled, lost and confused until you are able to love Him.

Loving your Creator completes you, His creation. Your relationship with the Lord is tolerable at best without an engaging and loving relationship. Loving the Lord moves you out of the basement of embarrassment to the balcony of basking in His presence.

Love lifts you to the Lord and He is drawn to your love. He loves to be loved by His children. It is love of the Lord that starts you out in your faith and sustains your faith. Loving the Lord fuels your faith, energizes your soul and galvanizes your beliefs.

It enflames hope and feeds forgiveness. Furthermore, loving the Lord is a catalyst for becoming more like Him. You take on the traits of whom and what you love. You are a reflection of the objects of your affections. Therefore, love Him, because you want to be like Him.

Transformation into the character of Christ is the goal for those who love Him. So, love the Lord with your whole being. Love Him with your body, soul and spirit. Love Him physically by taking care of the body He created. Keep it pure and healthy.

Love Him emotionally by processing and expressing your feelings. Allow Him to convert your anger into holy passion. Allow your love for Him to explode in the emotion of thanksgiving, praise and celebration.

Moreover, love Him with your spirit. Connect with Christ in prayer and meditation on His Word. He reveals His will for seeking souls, so love Him in the morning, in the noon-time and love Him when the sun goes down. Since loving Him is right, you don't want to be wrong.

Therefore, love the Lord without ceasing. Execute His greatest commandment by loving your Lover. He loves us so we can love Him!

What are some practical ways I can love Jesus with my heart and mind?

Related Readings: Deuteronomy 6:5; Joshua 23:11; 1 John 3:17; 5:1-3

27

Loving Lord

Because of the Lord's great love we are not consumed, for his compassions never
fail. They are new every morning; great is your faithfulness. I say to myself,
"The Lord is my portion; therefore I will wait for him."
Jeremiah 3:22-24

The love of God keeps you from being consumed by the fiery flames of grief. Your
sorrows can overwhelm you, but He is there as your loving heavenly Father to see you
through your sadness. The love of God is a peacemaker when you become consumed
with conflict.

His love mediates and works out solutions for all willing parties. Pride melts under the
loving influence of God. Worry is consuming until it comes under the direct influence
of God's love, for His love exudes peace. Thus, the peace of God and the worry of the
world cannot coexist. Fear can be all consuming, however, the love of God flushes out
fear and replaces it with trust.

The love of God floods your soul with faith, and fear vanquishes under its influence.
His compassions never fail for God has a deep awareness and concern for your
heartache. His compassions never fail for they give hope you can hang on to for future
resolution.

His compassions never fail for they provide companionship with your friend Jesus. His
compassions never fail for they extend forgiveness to a contrite and hurting heart. His
compassions solicit a successful soul. Great is His faithfulness. His faithfulness is
greater than the depths of the sea (six miles at its deepest point), and it is greater than
the highest mountain (six miles at its highest point).

The entire universe cannot contain the faithfulness of God, for it is far-reaching and
deep. People will fail you, but God is still faithful. Work will fail you, but God is still
faithful. Your health will fail you, but God is still faithful.

Finances will fail you, but God is still faithful. Circumstances will fail you, but God is still faithful. You will fail, but God is still faithful. He does what He says He will do, so you do not ever have to second-guess the Lord. He is there for you, your family, your friends and your enemies. He is faithful. He cannot, not be faithful.

For God to not be faithful would be like the sun not to rise, or the moon not to shine. This is not possible, just as it is impossible for God to be unfaithful. He will be faithful to lead you to the right spouse, the right career, and the right friends.

He can be trusted, so let go of your inhibitions and trust Him. You can trust Him with your future, your health, and your eternity. Therefore, wait on him for He is worth the wait. Use the opportunity of waiting to trust and obey Him, the Bible teaches, "I wait for your salvation, O LORD, and I follow your commands" (Psalm 119:166).

How does the Lord want me to trust Him, based on His great love and faithfulness from my past experiences and based on His promises?

Related Readings: 1 Kings 10:9; 2 Chronicles 7:6; 1 John 4:8-16

28

Parents Love Children

Then our sons in their youth will be like well-nurtured plants,
and our daughters will be like pillars carved to adorn a palace.
Psalm 144:12

Sons and daughters who seek the Lord grow in grace and mature in Christ. It brings great joy to parents when they see their children fall in love with Jesus. Their love for the Lord does not compete with, but compliments their devotion to their mother and father.

A mom nurtures her children, and a dad trains his teenagers. One encourages and the other exhorts. Moms care for their young, and dads lead them into young adulthood. Like a well-groomed plant the roots of our offspring need the soil of security in Jesus.

The watering of God's word keeps them healthy and growing. The warm sunlight of love, and the air of prayer keep them hopeful and alive, so make your home a hot house for heaven.

"I am reminded of your sincere faith, which first lived in your grandmother Lois and in your mother Eunice and, I am persuaded, now lives in you also" (2 Timothy 1:5).

However, sons and daughters do not always sing hymns and attend church. Sometimes they seek to find themselves outside the confines of Christ, and the protection of their parents. When they walk away from wisdom and find foolishness, what is a parent to do?

You love them in spite of their sorry selections. You express disappointment, but you determine to love them even more. You increase your prayers, and you invite them to play. Relationship is the lubricant the Lord uses to oil their hinges of obedience.

"Fathers, do not exasperate your children; instead, bring them up in the training and instruction of the Lord" (Ephesians 6:4).

Sons and daughters astray do not need to hear a sermon from mom and dad, but they do need to feel unconditional love and acceptance. Thank God for your sons and daughters. Seek to understand how the Lord has made them, and then love them at their point of uniqueness.

No child has ever complained about too much love, so love them to the Lord and He will work wonders in their hearts and minds. The Bible says, "He who fears the LORD has a secure fortress, and for his children it will be a refuge" (Proverbs 14:26).

How can I love my children like the Lord loves them?

Related Readings: Psalm 103:17; Proverbs 13:24; Hosea 11:4; 2 John 1:1

29

Unwise Love

No servant can serve two masters. Either he will hate the one and love the other, or he will be devoted to the one and despise the other. You cannot serve both God and Money. The Pharisees, who loved money, heard all this and were sneering at Jesus. He said to ther "You are the ones who justify yourselves in the eyes of men, but God knows your hearts. What is highly valued among men is detestable in God's sight."
Luke 16:13-15

There is a servitude that accompanies the love of God or the love of money for we serve what we love. In the case of Christ and cash you cannot serve both at the same time. The service of one cancels out the service of the other. It is the subtle service of money that short circuits service to my Savior Jesus.

I cannot love Him and stuff at the same time, Jesus says, "I will hate the one and love the other". If we are not careful our actions build an altar to the almighty dollar, and we ignore Almighty God, unless things go wrong and then we long for the Lord, our first love.

Holy God is jealous over love affairs outside of Himself, especially when money becomes our mistress, a demanding one at that. Jesus says love of money replaces love for Him, so how do you know if you are unfaithful? To defend or justify excessive amounts of time thinking or worrying about money is a sure bet it has captured your love.

To scheme about, manipulate for more, or be consumed with running out makes you a likely candidate for a lover of money. However, there is a remedy for our love affair with stuff, and that is to give it away.

"Command those who are rich in this present world not to be arrogant nor to put their hope in wealth, which is so uncertain, but to put their hope in God, who richly provides us with everything for our enjoyment. Command them to do good, to be rich in good deeds, and to be generous and willing to share. In this way they will lay up treasure for themselves as a firm foundation for the coming age, so that they may take hold of the life that is truly life" (1 Timothy 6:17-19).

Replace getting with giving, and then your love of God and people will excommunicate your love/hate relationship with money. Generosity frees you from being owned by money, and cash cannot control what it does not have. Make money a servant of your Savior Jesus, and you will certainly serve Him in the process. The reason many financially poor followers of Christ are faithful and free is because money has not become their master. Therefore, go with Christ over cash and you will find fulfillment, peace and contentment.

The Bible says, "For the love of money is a root of all kinds of evil. Some people, eager for money, have wandered from the faith and pierced themselves with many griefs" (I Timothy 6:10).

How can I increase my love for God and eradicate my love of money?

Related Readings: Proverbs 22:1; Colossians 3:1-10; 1 John 5:1-2

30

Sensitive Spouse

While Pilate was sitting on the judge's seat, his wife sent him this message:
"Don't have anything to do with that innocent man, for I have suffered
a great deal today in a dream because of him."
Matthew 27:19

Smart is the spouse who is sensitive to his or her spouse. God placed your husband or wife in your life to speak His thoughts through them.. This doesn't mean every word from a marriage partner is gospel, but it does mean we are wise if we listen to their admonishments. Suggestions from your spouse are not to be slighted, but taken seriously.

Rarely have I suffered harm by taking my wife's advice, but many times have I travailed for not trusting her instincts. Does your spouse know about the financial decision you are considering? Even if they are not interested, you honor them by asking for their input and keeping them informed of the facts. A sensitive spouse takes the time to communicate.

"The way of fools seems right to them, but the wise listen to advice." Proverbs 12:15

The concerns of a spouse may subside once they have time to prayerfully process the data, and get to know and trust those who are involved. It takes faith and patience to prolong the process, but it will lead to the best decision. Waiting takes the weight of the decision off you, and allows other godly advisors to get involved.

Create a habit of going to the Lord first and to your spouse second. If you are afraid of what either might think then recognize this is a sign to listen intently. Thank the Lord for a spouse who cares enough to speak up when they are concerned. Listen to them and love them through the process with prayer and collaboration. Christ gave you a sensitive spouse, so you can learn to be sensitive to them and to Him.

"However, each one of you also must love his wife as he loves himself, and the wife must respect her husband" (Ephesians 5:33).

What decision am I currently contemplating where I need to invite my spouse's input?

Related Readings: Exodus 18:19; Proverbs 19:20; Jeremiah 38:15; Acts 27:11

WHAT READERS ARE SAYING
ABOUT WISDOM HUNTERS

Thanks so much for this wisdom of truth. Sometimes I am weary of all the requests for things etc, but not God. For me this is a keeper to be looked at and read until I know it by heart. Thank you! – Ken

I really appreciate the Word today. I know God is in control but I always forget it. This spoke to me today in a way I've not experienced before. – Jen

Your message today really blessed my heart. It is a confirmation of where God has me. This is but a season for me, and sometimes it is difficult for us to recognize when we are in a season. Your prayer was just perfect for me as well. Thank you for allowing God to use you to minister and speak his word to me. It is a Blessing to my spirit. – Socratif

There are so many golden nuggets in your devotion this morning Brother Boyd...but ohhh the one..."TASTE HIS GRACE"...just fills my soul! God bless you. – Jenny

Thank you, Mr. Bailey, for Wisdom Hunters. I read it on my email as much as I can. It is so uplifting and I love that you list other Scriptures to follow-up with that days online message. God bless you in your work. Your sister in Christ. – Carol

I liked the devotional today, to make us of windows of opportunities that God has given to me. Thank you for this post and the other daily posts, it reaffirms my faith and makes me make right choices as I obey to His word. May God bless you and your family and all believers who are a part of this ministry. God bless you all. – Jonathan

I'm very grateful to have this resource. These devotionals provide biblical truth appropriate to current situations. They help me to hunger for more of God's word in my daily walk. Thank you for being such an encouraging reminder that God really cares, wants the best for us and he has our backs and all we have to do is walk in faithful obedience. – Noemi

I don't know how often I've turned to one of these messages and found just the words either I our someone I've been posting for has needed right in front of me. I'm truly blessed some nights using my phone as a flashlight and seeing just what I need to read, guiding my pathway!

Every morning I share this with my husband. This morning he left for his annual mission trip. At this time in my life I am staying home to take care of our children. Though only gone 10 days a year this morning I was quite frankly jealous. Jealous that he gets the glory, I the mundane. He the travel me the same routine. How dare he? Then I read this… Thank you Father for this reminder… I am truly grateful that my spouse gets to serve..and if I am patient my service is just as important. After all in 6 to 8 years WE will be going full time and living there together to serve.

How do you know where to minister to me each day? God uses your daily post to encourage me so much! Thank you. I am weary and you point me to the Living Water. God bless you mightily!

Dear Wisdom Hunters, I have been recieving your devotions for over a year now, and they have truly been a blessing to me as well as my friends and family that I forward them to. It seems like the writer knows exactly what is going on in my life. I know God is speaking to me through these devotions. My husband and I are going through some very difficult times right now and the only thing that has kept me going is the inspirational encouragement that I recieve through Wisdom Hunters. I just want to thank you. God is moving through your words which is being sent all over the US. God bless you!!

This devo was a "God-thing"!! I had been resisting calling a younger woman to take her out to lunch, out of fear. I finally obeyed God's leading, and the day I was going to meet her, I saw this devo. Amazing timing. Thank you so much for your ministry and faithfulness to God's calling – I have been inspired many times by your devotionals. God's richest blessing on you and your ministry!

BECOMING A DISCIPLE
OF JESUS CHRIST

My journey that led me to God covered a span of 19 years, before I truly understood my need for His love and forgiveness in a personal relationship with Jesus Christ. Along this path of spiritual awakening, God placed many people along the way as spiritual guideposts directing me toward Him.

Initially it was my mother who took me to church at age 12 so I could learn about faith through the confirmation process. My grandmother was a role model in her walk with Jesus by being kind and generous to all she encountered. Once in college, I began attending church with Rita (my future wife) and her family.

It was then that relevant weekly teaching from an ancient book—the Bible—began to answer many of life's questions. It intrigued me: What is God's plan for my life? Who is Jesus Christ? What are sin, salvation, heaven and hell? How can I live an - abundant life of forgiveness, joy and love?

So, the Lord found me first with His incredible love and when I surrendered in repentance and faith in Jesus, I found Him. For two years a businessman in our church showed me how to grow in grace through Bible study, prayer, faith sharing and service to others. I still discover each day more of God's great love and His new mercies.

Below is an outline for finding God and becoming a disciple of Jesus:

1. BELIEVE: "If you declare with your mouth, "Jesus is Lord," and believe in your heart that God raised him from the dead, you will be saved" (Romans 10:9). Belief in Jesus Christ as your Savior and Lord gives you eternal life in heaven.

2. REPENT AND BE BAPTIZED: "Peter replied, 'Repent and be baptized, every one of you, in the name of Jesus Christ for the forgiveness of your sins. And you will receive the gift of the Holy Spirit'" (Acts 2:38). Repentance means you turn from your sin and publically confess Christ in baptism.

3. OBEY: "Jesus replied, 'Anyone who loves me will obey my teaching. My Father will love them, and we will come to them and make our home with them'" (John 14:23). Obedience is an indicator of our love for the Lord Jesus and His presence in our life.

4. WORSHIP, PRAYER, COMMUNITY, EVANGELISM AND STUDY: "Every day they continued to meet together in the temple courts. They broke bread in their homes and ate together with glad and sincere hearts, praising God and enjoying the favor of all the people. And the Lord added to their number daily those who were being saved" (Acts 2:46-47). Worship and prayer are our expressions of gratitude and honor to God and our dependence on His grace. Community and evangelism are our accountability to Christians and compassion for non-Christians. Study to apply the knowledge, understanding, and wisdom of God.

5. LOVE GOD: "Jesus replied: 'Love the Lord your God with all your heart and with all your soul and with all your mind.' This is the first and greatest commandment" (Matthew 22:37-38). Intimacy with the almighty God is a growing and loving relationship. We are loved by Him, so we can love others and be empowered by the Holy Spirit to obey His commands.

6. LOVE PEOPLE: "And the second is like it: 'Love your neighbor as yourself'" (Matthew 22:39). Loving people is an outflow of the love for our heavenly Father. We are able to love because He first loved us.

7. MAKE DISCIPLES: "And the things you have heard me say in the presence of many witnesses entrust to reliable people who will also be qualified to teach others" (2 Timothy 2:2). The reason we disciple others is because we are extremely grateful to God and to those who disciple us, and we want to obey Christ's last instructions before going to heaven.

Daily Wisdom in Your Inbox... A Free Subscription: www.wisdomhunters.com

MEET THE AUTHOR

Boyd Bailey

Boyd Bailey, the author of Wisdom Hunters devotionals, is the founder of Wisdom Hunters, Inc., an Atlanta-based ministry created to encourage Christians (a.k.a wisdom hunters) to *apply God's unchanging Truth in a changing world*.

By God's grace, Boyd has impacted wisdom hunters in over 86 countries across the globe through the Wisdom Hunters daily devotion, wisdomhunters.com devotional blog and devotional books.

For over 30 years Boyd Bailey has passionately pursued wisdom through his career in fulltime ministry, executive coaching, and mentoring.

Since becoming a Christian at the age of 19, Boyd begins each day as a wisdom hunter, diligently searching for Truth in scripture, and through God's grace, applying it to his life.

These raw, 'real time' reflections from his personal time with the Lord, are now impacting over 111,000 people through the Wisdom Hunters Daily Devotion email. In addition to the daily devotion, Boyd has authored nine devotional books: *Infusion*, a 90-day devotional, *Seeking Daily the Heart of God Vol I & II*, 365-day devotionals *Seeking God in the Proverbs*, a 90-day devotional and *Seeking God in the Psalms*, a 90-day devotional along with several 30-day devotional e-Books on topics such as *Wisdom for Fathers*, *Wisdom for Mothers*, *Wisdom for Graduates*, and *Wisdom for Marriage*.

In addition to Wisdom Hunters, Boyd is the co-founder and CEO of Ministry Ventures, a faith based non-profit, where he has trained and coached over 1000 ministries in the best practices of prayer, board, ministry models, administration and fundraising. Prior to Ministry Ventures, Boyd was the National Director for Crown Financial Ministries and an Associate Pastor at First Baptist Church of Atlanta. Boyd serves on numerous boards including Ministry Ventures, Wisdom Hunters, Atlanta Mission, Souly Business and Blue Print for Life.

Boyd received his Bachelor of Arts from Jacksonville State University and his Masters of Divinity from Southwestern Seminary. He and Rita, his wife of 30 plus years, live in Roswell, Georgia and are blessed with four daughters, three sons-in-law who love Jesus, two granddaughters and two grandsons. Boyd and Rita enjoy missions and investing in young couples, as well as hiking, reading, traveling, working through their bucket list, watching college football, and hanging out with their kids and grand kids when ever possible.